One, Two, Three, Pooph!!!

Reopen Country Now!

Return to normalcy is just around the corner.

After the big nightmare that seemed to never end, Americans do not need 50 Governors' extending the goal line. Perhaps Congress should give up their paychecks to get the right taste in its mouth.

Unfortunately, in my twenties, I registered Democrat. I now am sure that Democrat leadership does not care about me or any regular people. the people. One recent example is they would have unanimously reauthorized the $2.5 billion requested by the SBA for all the John Does in America. Some of my family members benefited but the program's funding ran out because it the Democrats refused to increase the SBA funding. I rest my case.

The verdict is in, Democrats in leadership positions such as governors, have been fighting to keep America locked down while their constituencies are starving looking to get back to work. Why? Can it be they think a better economy it would help Trump get reelected. Is that why Congress ran out of town and are hiding.

So what can we do? Impeach every governor who keeps us locked at home? Maybe! In this book we tell you about how to ignore the negative pleadings of the Democrat leaders and instead work to release the yoke upon America and its economy. Let's open her up all at once, protect ourselves from the virus w/o government intervention and let's make it all good. Brian Kelly wrote this book to show us all how to get it done.

LETS GO PUBLISH

I0025828

BRIAN W. KELLY

Copyright 2020 Brian W. Kelly   Editor, Brian P. Kelly
Title: **One, Two, Three, Pooph!!!**   Author Brian W. Kelly
Subtitle: **Reopen Country Now!**
       Return to normalcy is just around the corner.

Published by: LETS GO PUBLISH!
Publisher: Brian P. Kelly
Editor: Brian P. Kelly
P.O Box 621   Wilkes-Barre, PA   www.letsgopublish.com

Library of Congress Copyright Information Pending
Book Cover Design by Brian W. Kelly;
Editing by Brian P. Kelly

ISBN Information: The International Standard Book Number (ISBN) is a unique machine-readable identification number, which marks any book unmistakably. The ISBN is the clear standard in the book industry. 159 countries and territories are officially ISBN members. The Official ISBN For this book is also on the outside cover: **978-1-951562-20-5**

The price for this work is: **$10.95 USD**

10   9   8   7   6   5   4   3   2   1

Release Date: May 2020

LETS
GO
PUBLISH!

Dedication

I dedicate this book to all of the great health care workers and first responders. I am talking about the great heroes of the coronavirus pandemic from doctors, nurses, lab technicians, bus drivers, truck drivers, cafeteria workers and you know who else. God bless you and thank you for your great assistance during the Coronavirus crisis. We all appreciate your great work and your bravery in fighting a tough virus.

Thank You All!

Acknowledgments

I appreciate all the help that I have received in putting this book together as well as all of my other 233 other published books.

My printed acknowledgments had become so large that book readers "complained" about going through too many pages to get to page one of the text.

And, so to permit me more flexibility, I put my acknowledgment list online, and it continues to grow. Believe it or not, it once cost about a dollar more to print each book.

Thank you and God bless you all for your help.

Please check out www.letsgopublish.com to read the latest version of my heartfelt acknowledgments updated for this book. FYI, Wily Ky Eyely loves this book and recommends it to all.

Click the bottom of the Main menu on the web site!

Thank you all!

Preface:

Rarely does a book title explain exactly what a book is about. This book is the exception. This book does not explain in detail the rationale behind the virus, the cause, but it offers some information about how to prevent it and to cure it. There is no question about it. The essence of this book is the recommendation to the President for the best way to restart the economy.

After the 2020 coronavirus nightmare that seemed to never end, the last thing Americans need now is 50 Governors extending the goal line. Yet that is what our officials, mostly Democrats. Perhaps Congress should give up their paychecks for the duration.

My brother Joseph has a great saying when nobody is listening to his suggestions. After a short while, he raises his hand and says, Talk to the Hand. He goes into a disinterested mode and often gets a positive rise out of his adversary. I wish my brother were an American official right now. He was once a top manager in the VA and he under stands people. Unfortunately, he learned in his time on the job that our adversaries have no shame.

I am a Democrat. As A Democrat, I know that Democrat leadership does not care about the people. They would have by unanimous consent reauthorized the $2.5 billion requested by the SBA. My family members benefitted from that but the programs funding ran out because it was helping small businesses as expected. Democrats refused to increase the SBA funding. I rest my case.

Democrats, one by one in leadership positions such as governors do not want America reopened or the economy restarted. Why? They think it would help Trump get reelected. Thats why the Congress has run out of Washington and are hiding. They no longer represent the people and the Dems are actually for the socialists and not the normal Americans.

So what to do? In this book we tell you about how to ignore the negative pleadings of the Democrat leaders and instead work to release the yoke upon America and its economy. Lets open up and lets make it good. Read this book to know how to get it done.

Why did Brian W. Kelly write this book?

Brian W. Kelly wrote this book because he cares about the United States and the other countries affected by this nasty virus. I am publishing this book because I care.

I hope you enjoy this book and I hope that it inspires you to take the individual actions necessary to help yourself during this pandemic crisis. I am convinced that if you follow the guidance herein we can all emerge better than ever.

Government should be a helpful tool in solving this deep moral and potentially existential dilemma for our country. Don't always believe the Democrats when they say "no" to something you know makes sense.

I wish you the best.

Brian P. Kelly, Publisher
Wilkes-Barre, Pennsylvania

Table of Contents:

About the Author

Brian W. Kelly retired as an Assistant Professor in the Business Information Technology (BIT) program at Marywood University, where he also served as the IBM i and Midrange Systems Technical Advisor to the IT Faculty. Kelly designed, developed, and taught many college and professional courses. He continues as a contributing technical editor to a number of IT industry magazines, including "The Four Hundred" and "Four Hundred Guru," published by IT Jungle.

Kelly is a former IBM Senior Systems Engineer and IBM Mid Atlantic Area Specialist. His specialty was designing applications for customers as well as implementing advanced IBM operating systems and software facilities on their machines.

He has an active information technology consultancy. He is the author of 233 books and numerous technical articles. Kelly has been a frequent speaker at COMMON, IBM conferences, and other technical conferences.

Brian was a candidate for US Congress from Pennsylvania in 2010 and he brings a lot of experience to his writing endeavors.

Brian Kelly knows that the Pandemic crisis can be solved with the right therapeutic in the short term as soon as we can get officials to open up the country. People will make the right decisions

Chapter 1 The President's Plan for Reopening.

President Trump takes questions from the press April 16, 2020

On April 16, 2020 President Trump addressed the nation at 6:00 PM to unveil the nation's new plan to reopen the country. I think it is too complicated but with the Executive Branch working hard to make it happen, I'd say it has a good chance. I have my one citizen-centric plan that I think is much easier. It begins after the summary of the phased plan for the nation in the last chapter.

What is in the WH game plan?

The administration's 18-page guidance document details three phases to reopen state economies, with each phase lasting, at minimum, 14 days. The guidelines in full can be seen here: https://www.whitehouse.gov/openingamerica/

You can get a printout of the complete guidelines in your local paper if you do not have an Internet account.

The plans include some recommendations across all three phases including good personal hygiene and employers developing policies to ensure social distancing, testing and contact tracing.

Phase one includes much of the current lockdown measures such as avoiding non-essential travel and not gathering in groups. But it says large venues such as restaurants, places of worship and sports venues "can operate under strict physical distancing protocols".

If there is no evidence of a resurgence of the coronavirus, phase two allows non-essential travel to resume. The guidance says schools can reopen and bars can operate "with diminished standing-room occupancy".

Under phase three, states which are still seeing a downward trend of symptoms and cases can allow "public interactions" with physical distancing and the unrestricted staffing of worksites. Visits to care homes and hospitals can resume and bars can increase their standing room capacity.

Some regions could begin returning to normal after a month-long evaluation period, at the earliest, according to the document.
In places where there are more infections or where rates begin to rise, it could take longer.

The coordinator of the White House coronavirus task force, Dr Deborah Birx, told Thursday's briefing that as states worked through the three phases, they could allow for more and more employees to return to work in increments.

Phase three would be the "new normal", she said, and would still include suggestions that vulnerable people should avoid crowded spaces.

My personal plan to shut-down the coronavirus & return to normalcy is highlighted in the last chapter. In essence, the best summary of my plan was given by Dr. Fauci as the way NOT to reopen.

"Pull the light switch ASAP. This plan gets rid of facemasks, scrubbing hands, & social distancing at bars & opens up a fun America with proper caution. It's time!"

So what to do? In this book we tell you about how to ignore the negative pleadings of the Democrat leaders and instead work to release the yoke upon America and its economy. Lets open up and lets make it good. My suggestion is that you read this book to know how to get it done.

This 2020 coronavirus nightmare sill seems to never want to end. At least officials in blue states do not want it to end. Despite the last thing that Americans needed was 50 Governors extending the goal line, that is exactly what our officials, mostly Democrats did to us. Perhaps Congress should give up their paychecks for the duration.

I admit that I am a Democrat—a JFK conservative Democrat. As such, I know that Democrat leadership does not care about the people. They would have by unanimous consent reauthorized the $2.5 billion requested by the SBA if they cared. My family members benefited from that but the programs funding ran out because it was helping small businesses as expected. Democrats refused to increase the SBA funding. I rest my case.

Democrats, one by one in leadership positions such as governors, still do not want America reopened or the economy restarted. Why? They think it would help Trump get reelected. That' s why the Congress has run out of Washington and are hiding. They no longer represent the people and the Dems are actually for the socialists and not the normal Americans.

Experts and non-experts alike are offering their thoughts on the issue of reopening or listening to government officials. Here is what Ron Paul has to say about it:

Former Congressional Representative Ron Paul Asks" What if the 'cure' is worse than the disease?

http://ronpaulinstitute.org/

From California to New Jersey, Americans are protesting in the streets. They are demanding an end to house arrest orders given by government officials over a virus outbreak that even according to the latest U.S. government numbers will claim fewer lives than the seasonal flu outbreak of 2017-18.

Across the U.S., millions of businesses have been shut down by "executive order" and the unemployment rate has skyrocketed to levels not seen since the Great Depression. Americans, who have seen their real wages decline thanks to Federal Reserve monetary malpractice, are finding themselves thrust into poverty and standing in breadlines. It is like a horror movie, but it's real.

Dr. Ron Paul

Last week, the UN Secretary General warned that a global recession resulting from the worldwide coronavirus lockdown could cause "hundreds of thousands of additional child deaths per year."

As of this writing, less than 170,000 have been reported to have died from the coronavirus worldwide.

Many Americans have also died this past month because
they were not able to get the medical care they needed.
Cancer treatments have been indefinitely postponed. Life-
saving surgeries have been put off to make room for
coronavirus cases. Meanwhile hospitals are laying off
thousands because the expected coronavirus cases have not
come and the hospitals are partially empty.

What if the "cure" is worse than the disease?

Countries like Sweden that did not lock down their economy
and place the population under house arrest are faring no
worse than countries that did. Sweden's deaths-per-million
from coronavirus is lower than in many lockdown countries.

Likewise, U.S. states that did not arrest citizens for merely
walking on the beach are not doing worse than those that

did. South Dakota governor Kristi Noem said last week, "We've been able to keep our businesses open and allow people to take on some personal responsibility." South Dakota has recorded a total of seven coronavirus deaths.

Kentucky, a strict lockdown state, is five times more populated than South Dakota, yet it has some 20 times more coronavirus deaths. If lockdown and house arrest are the answer, shouldn't those numbers be reversed, with South Dakota seeing mass death while Kentucky dodges the coronavirus bullet?

When Dr. Anthony Fauci first warned that two million would die, there was a race among federal, state and local officials to see who could rip up the Constitution fastest. Then Fauci told us if we do what he says only a quarter of a million would die. They locked America down even harder. Then, with little more than a shrug of the shoulders, they announced that a maximum of 60,000 would die, but maybe less. That is certainly terrible, but it's just a high-average flu season.

Imagine if we had used even a fraction of the resources spent to lock down the entire population and focused on providing assistance and protection to the most vulnerable – the elderly and those with serious medical conditions. We could have protected these people and still had an economy to go back to when the virus had run its course. And it wouldn't have cost us $6 trillion, either.

Governments have no right or authority to tell us what business or other activity is "essential." Only in totalitarian states does the government claim this authority. We should encourage all those who are standing up peacefully and demanding an accounting from their elected leaders. They should not be able to get away with this.

--- end of Ron Paul Essay ---

Chapter 2 Mitigation Helps...But...

Does all of the mitigation stop the spread of the virus and protect the people? Governor Andrew Cuomo was shocked when he discovered the answer to that question as he examined the data in New York. Cuomo says it's 'shocking' most new coronavirus hospitalizations are people who had been staying home. So, maybe the right approach is that we ought to just let the businesses and the people make their best decisions.

Maybe we should keep government out of making decisions for the people.

What would you conclude?

23,000 high schools, 5300 colleges and universities equals 28,300 valedictorians

Here we are, the people of America, forced to be locked up in our own homes while our non-medical expert governors decide when, if ever, we get to go out again and we get our Constitution back. There are a lot of smart people in our country. When people go to school, most of the time, they get even smarter.

For example, there are 23,000 high schools and 5300 colleges and universities in the United States. If we consider that together this is 28,300 learning institutions, we know each year at graduation each one of these institutions has at least one valedictorian, aka the smartest person in the school. That is a lot of smart people.

We know from our own life experiences and the schools we attended that the valedictorian (s) is the student usually having the highest rank in a graduating class who delivers the valedictory address at the commencement exercises.

Is either Tony Fauci or Deborah Birx among the smartest people in the world? Not to put them down but we do not know. Were they valedictorians. What we do know is that there are a lot of smart people and not all have been motivated to achieve valedictorian status. These people are like us in a lot of ways except they may opt to take matters further than we might in coming to a rational conclusion. The coronavirus gives fodder for a lot of original thinking, don't you think?

Smart people today continue to come to their own conclusions about matters in which our coronavirus experts believe they are the "end-all." I have two such smart people in my life that I would like to introduce you to. One is named Dennis and one is named Al. I know them both and if they were not valedictorians, they should have been.

They have a lot to say about the predicament in which we find ourselves today. In Chapter 8, we will first hear from Dennis who hits the nail on the head in this short essay titled:

Coronavirus' generally held views that happen to be wrong.

Check it out in the prelude to the last chapter. You'll like it.!

Chapter 3 Phased Reopening Plan Controlled by the States

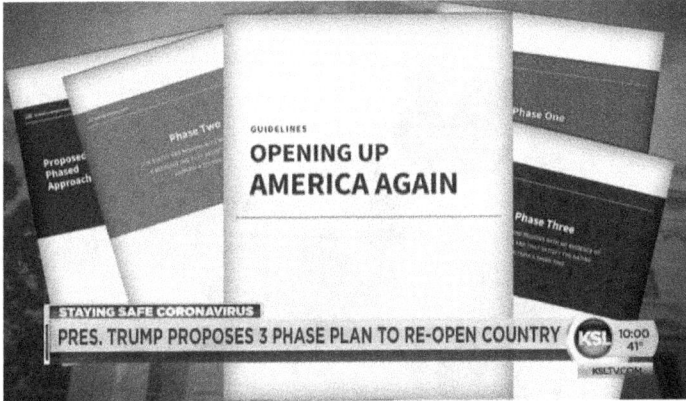

The President announced that any state can start reopening while acknowledging the decision is theirs. The guidelines released by the president effectively mean that any restoration of American society will take place on a patchwork basis. There can be as many as fifty patches—one for each state. States also have the latitude to direct counties in their state to follow different guidelines rather than big and small counties having to operate the same.

It helps to understand that the task force produced guidelines. Most states it is expected, will adhere to the guidelines but strict adherence is not mandated.

Trump has been talking about a reopening America for several weeks. He telegraphed his desire to restart the economy several weeks ago and April 16 was the date the guidelines were released.

In internal documents, federal health officials warn that the bar to do so safely may be too high. We wonder if Trump is in charge sometimes as these Federal health officials have a lot of power to warn leaders on the "White House's coronavirus task force" of their concerns. This week all members of the task force and a special group tasked with creating guidelines for the reopening of America, completed their guidelines.

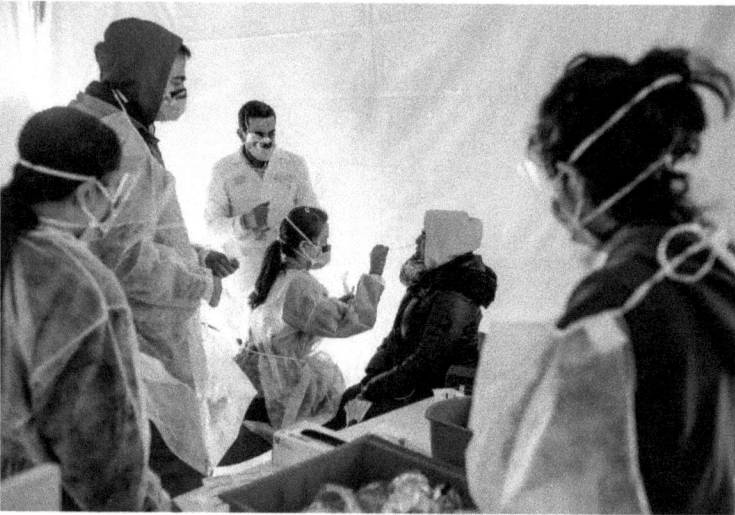

They noted that reopening the nation will require a massive capacity to test, track and treat people for the ongoing threat of the novel coronavirus.

President Trump suggested early in the week of April 16 that "It's going to be very, very soon," President Trump said at a press conference Tuesday, "sooner than the end of the month." On April 16, he announced his plan in which the states call the shots. The plan is generalized throughout the book and there is also a link to the 18 page plan in chapter 1. The best plan of action is described in the last chapter of this book.

The people are saying, "Enough is Enough… We are not children. We are adults. Most adults will make the right decisions."

Protests are erupting in typically quiet states. Besides that, businesses have decided to reopen in US without official permission in defiance of lockdowns. The people believe The Constitution is their empowerment.

POOPH! Can the economy magically come back on its own?

Even though it is hard to believe, businesses across the US are reopening daily despite shutdown orders as the backlash continues against strict stay-at-home orders to fight the coronavirus pandemic.

Businesses from restaurants to hairstylists in states such as Pennsylvania, Illinois, and California and other parts of the US have already abandoned the lockdown and are doing their own thing despite continuing and toughening restrictions.

It comes as hundreds of flag-waving protesters gathered at the state government's buildings and along California beaches to protest closures.

In the California's capital, Sacramento, police lined steps outside the building, as protesters waved signs that said "Defend Freedom" and broke into "U-S-A" chants. The people are upset with the dictators having taken control of state governments,

In major defiance, many are not wearing face masks intended to deter spread of the virus.
In one California location, for example, a small plane circled overhead, displaying a banner carrying an image of California governor, Gavin Newsom's face and the slogan, "End his tyranny." The people are no longer standing by and taking it.

It is not pleasant out there folks. The people have had enough.

Chapter 4 Open Up America for Business

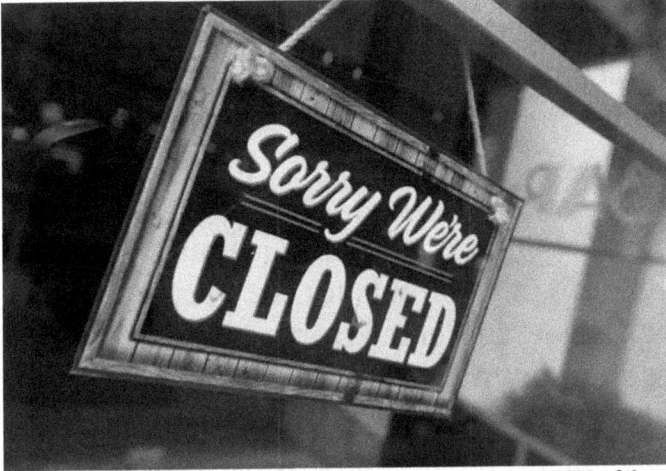

Times Square Establishment—A SIGN of the times

Introduction

After two months of formal shutdowns in the many of the states across the nation, the president announced his plan to restart life in America on April 16. Having lived through the social distancing and the lack of fun in America for all this time, families have actually had it up to here ⬆ with restrictions. With 36,000,000 unemployed as of last count before printing, the economy is not poised to come back soon and those interested in America surviving have been urging to get things started sooner rather than later.

And, so, I take no issue with the President's guidelines as guidelines. Along with other Americans, however, I take issue with the dictators in state capitals ignoring the constitution by extending lockdowns beyond the point of reasonable.

In the last chapter, you will find my simple plan which is based on the simple principle that the people can be trusted. I like my plan better than the imposed lockdowns. Nobody wants to die. Isn't that obvious. Thanks to government dictates, many in long term care facilities, thousands are already dead. My precepts are simple and are based on the feeling that I get from some people six feet away as I walk the neighborhood.

They include thoughts about the autocrats running our lives and making life much more miserable for the people than they must be. For example, in Pennsylvania the state run Liquor Stores were shut down until recently as most state residents were are coming to the end of their one month backup supply. I have heard during these walks by some unhappy travelers that it might be even better to get the virus and have the threat and the dictatorship end as most people do survive the illness.

I am not recommending this but governors can and should make this time as bearable for the people as possible. They are not making any friends that is one thing that is for sure.

Should we stay closed and separated?

On April 10, four days before I began this chapter for the first time, the New York Times Magazine wrote a piece about restarting America. After a read of their article one would not necessarily conclude that we should ever restart when government is being so helpful to the people right now.

Here is how they began their article:

"The politics of the coronavirus have made it seem indecent to talk about the future. As President Trump has flirted with reopening America quickly — saying in late March that he'd like to see "packed churches" on Easter and returning to the theme days ago with "we cannot let this continue" — public-health experts have felt compelled to call out the dangers. Many Americans have responded by rejecting as monstrous the whole idea of any trade-off between saving lives and saving the economy. And in the near term, it's true that those two goals align: For the sake of both, it's imperative to keep businesses shuttered and people in their homes as much as possible.

In the longer run, though, it's important to acknowledge that a trade-off will emerge — and become more urgent in the coming months, as the economy slides deeper into recession. The staggering toll of unemployment has reached more than 22 million in just the last four weeks. There will be difficult compromises between doing everything possible to save lives from COVID-19 and preventing other life-threatening, or - altering, harms.

When can the US ethically bring people back to work and school and begin to resume the usual rhythms of American life? The times brought five people together in a video-conference and asked them point blank, what would it take to reopen America. Of course there is the current battle of who has the authority—the President or the fifty Governors. But, assuming that one will be solved, there is a lot of disagreement on when we should open. For eight governors, in fact, who have not issued stay-at home orders, the opening question is moot. They have not shut down.

If you want to see what the Times says about the subject, feel free to go to

https://www.nytimes.com/2020/04/10/magazine/coronav
irus-economy-debate.html. The panelists in their piece do
not reflect my views on the subject.. Bioethicist Ezekiel
Emanuel adopted the "Whole Lives" program for
Obamacare. The "Death Panels" were part of his work in
which if you were under ten or above fifty years old,
Emanuel would serve you your health-care last.

Zeke would not be on my panel. He is not pro-American in
my opinion. His take is to keep America shut down until
there is a vaccine, which he believes will be here in perhaps
eighteen months. By then folks, if we stayed shut down with
enhanced social distancing as in Michigan, China would
own America. Therefore, I am not interested at all in the
Emanuel Plan.

What if you knew that the number of deaths from the flu this
year were more than four times the number of deaths from
the coronavirus. Would you be as worried. Would you think
this is much ado about nothing? It is by the way more than
four times that of COVID-19.

In the U.S. alone, the flu this year (also called influenza) has
caused an estimated 38 million illnesses, 390,000
hospitalizations and up to 62,000 deaths this season. Think
about that. It's like that every year and we do not close
down the country. COVID-19 has caused about 32,000
deaths in the US this year because we have no vaccine and
the experts won't accept the best therapeutic as our gold
standard—hydroxychloroquine. Many doctors swear that
the # of deaths would be significantly less if
hydroxychloroquine were adopted as both a prophylaxis and
as a possible cure.

President concerned about an Economic Collapse

President Donald Trump is a realist about public-health policies that could harm the economy and the American public. At this point of the pandemic, he sees the risk of economic collapse as a major potential cause for loss of life in the future—and not because of the flu or a virus.

Trump has attracted crucial allies among Republican leaders overseeing the movement of millions of Americans. People are sick of staying at home waiting for their businesses to be destroyed. They want to fight back rather than go down without a ship.

Florida Governor Ron DeSantis for a long time resisted enacting orders that would restrict people to their homes. His philosophy was unlike what other large states such as New York and California have done. Instead, his office has advised that people older than 65 should stay inside. DeSantis too gave in on April 1. When he announced the curtailment of businesses, he said the decision corresponded with the "national pause" effectively recommended by the White House. Governors of both parties made clear they will move at their own pace.,

Mississippi Governor Tate Reeves also balked, saying the state isn't China and the US has a Constitution. Alabama Governor Kay Ivey has said she has no plans for a state shelter-in-place order, so the City of Birmingham with a Dem Mayor approved its own Tuesday. Democrats at the city and state and national level sure do hate citizens having freedom.

Democrats are more interested in opposing Trump than helping America. If they can get away with doing nothing, that will be their approach. Democrats don't like business and they liken the shutdown to how things would be in a socialist country—so why change things by going back to work when that is exactly what Democrats do not want.

The billionaires on Wall Street are playing the hedge funds and other financial instruments and they are making tons of money while the rest of the country is hurting. Regular Americans believe that Wall Street is for Republicans but it is not so. The progressive liberal billionaires on the Street do not want the people to come back to work. They are making their billions without the people working.

And, so, the Wall Street types business leaders on the phone call with Trump on April 15, urged the President to dramatically increase coronavirus testing no matter how long the country has to shut down. During this first call to discuss reopening country, Wall Street big shot Democrats sided with DeWine and told the president more testing is needed to convince the public to return to work

We will discuss that and other factors of reopening the country in the next several chapters. Check out chapter 8 for the simple solution for reopening. No kidding!

Chapter 5 Can Anti-Virals Help?

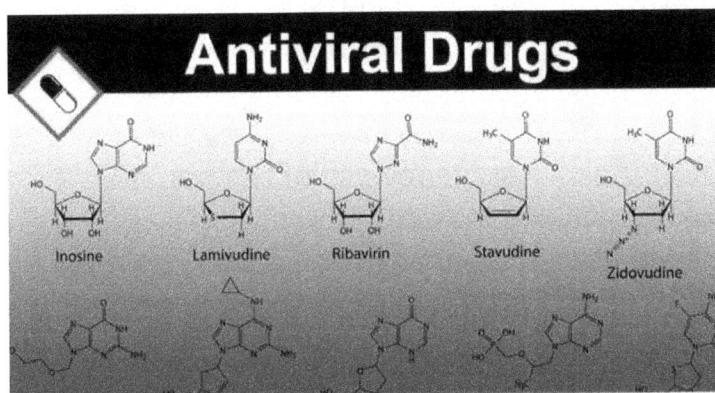

What do you do when you don't know? Hopefully when asked, you will admit that you do not know. Unfortunately, the media in the US uses a different standard. They want to know what Trump thinks about the answer to the question. If Trump says X, the media, without any research of their own know the answer intrinsically with no further study. They know that it is not X, and so it is Y, if there are just two options.

Using media logic, several weeks after I heard Dr. Oz and some pretty credentialed epidemiologists and cardiologists touting hydroxychloro-quine and even chloroquine as a game changer in the fight for a cure and a preventative (prophylaxis) for the coronavirus, I was very encouraged.

I began to study all I could (without being a doctor) to see if there was more than anecdotal evidence for the claim. Let me say that I learned that most doctors use the drug to treat themselves so they do not get infected and though that is not science, it is great news.

Moreover, in a recent global survey, Hydroxychloroquine was rated 'most effective therapy' by doctors for coronavirus. Yes, this drug, known for treating malaria is being used extensively by U.S. doctors mostly for high-risk COVID-19 patients.

The FDA has authorized emergency use of the malaria medicines for severely ill coronavirus patients who are already in the hospital. Emergency use is a lower bar than full-on approval. FDA full approval requires piles of clinical data about a drug's effectiveness and safety. Those answers are still in the works, and the FDA has acknowledged that even if the drugs are effective, doctors don't know the best dosing yet to treat the virus. However, the doctors have figured that out already by using it themselves. Moreover, they use it for more than just emergency use for COVID-19.

Chloroquine has been safely used since 1944 (about 65 years) as an antimalarial drug. Here is its full set of FDA approved uses

(1) For the treatment of uncomplicated malaria due to P. falciparum, P. malariae, P. ovale, and P. vivax.

(2) Chronic discoid lupus erythematosus and systemic lupus erythematosus in adults and

(3) Treatment of acute and chronic rheumatoid arthritis in adults.

The FDA recently posted information regarding worldwide shortages of hydroxychloroquine and chloroquine to its drug shortages webpage due to a significant surge in demand, notably as a result of US President Donald Trump's pronouncement that the drug could be a 'game changer' in the fight against COVID-19. This shortage is not good news and must be addressed quickly with the same dispatch as the N95 masks.

Trump already ordered a stockpile of 30 million doses but he needs to ramp up production to fulfill the need for using the drug as a prophylaxis and as a cure for COVID-19 when America reopens. The American population is in excess of 330,000,000.

Physicians use Hydroxychloroquine worldwide

Valerie Richardson of The Washington Times reported a week ago on Thursday, April 2, 2020 that an international poll of more than 6,000 doctors released Thursday found that the antimalarial drug hydroxychloroquine was the most highly rated treatment for the novel coronavirus. For me that means I want it if I am sick with the virus or as a prophylaxis.

The survey was conducted by Sermo, a global health care polling company, of 6,227 physicians in 30 countries. They found that 37% of those treating COVID-19 patients rated hydroxychloroquine as the "most effective therapy" from a list of 15 options. These are doctors.

Of the physicians surveyed, 3,308 said they had either ordered a COVID-19 test or been involved in caring for a coronavirus patient, and 2,171 of those responded to the question asking which medications were most effective. Only when the scientific community accepts information such as this and offers real opinions about the positive aspects of its efficacy will this treatment get the full respect that it deserves from the world. Then, many real lives will be saved.

The activist press is against hydroxychloroquine after finding out that from the daily briefings that President Donald Trump authorized Peter Navarro to find thirty million or more doses from around the world from countries who had chosen not to export the medicine. Navarro found them and brought them to the stockpile. If Trump is for anything, the activist press is against it for no other reason.

President Donald Trump has expressed his interest in the merits of the anti-malarial drug hydroxychloroquine as a coronavirus game changing cure and as a prophylaxis. I learned about it from two doctors on the Laura Ingraham show and the evidence is compelling

Drs. Ramin Oskoui, cardiologist and CEO of Foxhall cardiology, and Stephen Smith, founder of the Smith Center for Infectious Diseases and Urban Health, told their story to Laura Ingraham on Fox News. The activist opposition press refute all of the evidence presented because they fear a cure for the coronavirus would assure a victory for Trump in the November elections. It is amazing that this activist opposition media does not care what happens to America as long as they can discredit the President.

Democrat Representative cured by hydroxychloroquine

Despite the opinion of the lying press, nonetheless, former coronavirus patients like actor Daniel Dae Kim and Michigan Democrat State Representative Karen Whitsett swear by it. However, even after receiving emergency FDA approval, the anti-malarial drug hydroxychloroquine still has an image problem on the political left after being touted by President Trump. When the left found Trump favored the drug, that was enough for them to be against it—unless of course they get the virus.

Democratic State Representative Karen Whitsett from Michigan has been telling anybody who will listen about her good news. She says that the controversial drug hydroxychloroquine stopped her coronavirus symptoms "within a couple hours."

The FDA issued the emergency-use authorization late Sunday for chloroquine and its next-generation version, hydroxychloroquine, as treatments for the novel coronavirus, fueling the political back-and-forth that erupted March 19 when Mr. Trump called hydroxychloroquine a potential "game changer."

The latest information from early May 2020 is as follows:

Hydroxychloroquine (HCQ) was accepted as a COVID-19 treatment by the medical community in the US and worldwide by early April. 67% of the US physicians said they would prescribe HCQ or chloroquine CQ for COVID-19 to a family member (Town Hall, 2020-04-08).

An international poll of doctors rated HCQ the most effective coronavirus treatment (NY Post, 2020-04-02). On April 6, Peter Navarro told CNN that "Virtually Every COVID-19 Patient In New York Is Given Hydroxychloroquine." This might explain decrease in COVID-19 deaths in the New York state after April 15.

Chapter 6 Stories about Hydroxychloroquine

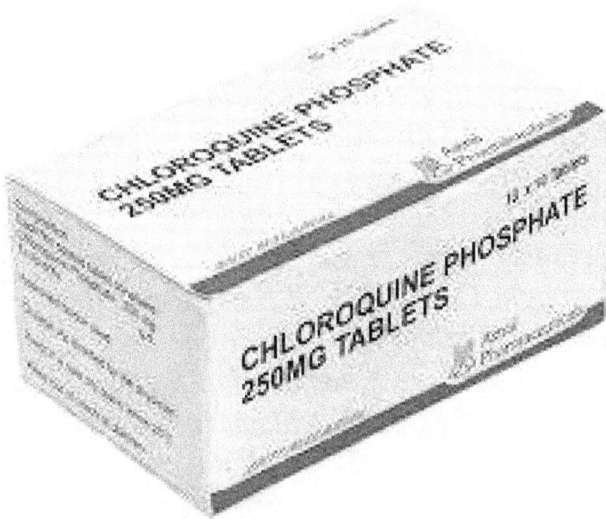

There is enough evidence for me that the drug is safe and effective as a cure and as a prophylaxis that I wrote two articles for my local paper. I was called the other day telling me that the first was about to be printed in the Citizens Voice.

With all of the fuss for the first month of the shutdown with hospitals and EMTs having mask shortages and doctors and nurses having to go to work without the proper PPE's (personal protective equipment, I penned this article

Here is the first Short Letter in italics that I sent to the editor.

Date: Wed, 25 Mar 2020 19:11:59 -0400
From: "Brian W. Kelly"
Subject: What if we no longer needed N95 masks?

I have no medical credentials to be considered but I offer this anyway.. My favorite poem by Emily Dickinson starts with I'm nobody, who are you? I know who I am.

In my whole career with IBM I was a problem solver. Problems that we did not know about yesterday, we had to solve today. When I get a problem in my head and possible solutions, I did not stop until my solution was proven wrong and I had to move on to possible solution #2, or 3, or whatever.

I am intrigued by the studied capabilities of hydroxychloroquine, an effective malaria drug to fight COVID-19. It is in clinical tests in NY since Tuesday but I hear nothing about it. In the French study that has been popularized by Dr. Oz, we know that the French have cured all members of their small study. It took one person a few days longer to show relaxed symptoms. But that person too was cured. Hydroxychloroquine is also seen as a great prophylaxis (preventative). It is used so that those heading to malaria infested countries do not contract malaria.

It is said anecdotally that it does the same for the coronavirus. In other words, it can prevent one from contracting the virus.

What if it works? Does anybody know? It seems like nobody at this point cares about its preventative abilities.

Think of it?

Until the major innovations in making N95 masks for hospital workers were developed, there was and there still may be a mask shortage.

What if hydroxychloroquine were such an effective prophylaxis for the virus that anybody who took the proper preventative dosage became immune from getting the virus?

What if?

How are problems solved but first with a thesis?

What if?

The N95 mask shortage would no longer matter if a simple pill or injection could prevent the virus from affecting hospital and other EMT workers.

Should we know more about this?

We could concentrate on respirators and testing!

--- End of letter ---

After a week, I added to the facts in the letter and sent another letter.

2nd letter to the editor about hydroxychloroquine

Date: Wed, 8 Apr 2020 07:11:34 -0400
From: "Brian W. Kelly"
Subject: Save lives with this new therapeutic remedy

Doctors themselves are taking chloroqine and hydroxychloroquine as a cure and as a prophylactic. The people should know about this.

Additionally, with the significant # of health care workers and EMS who have caught the virus in their work it would also help in keeping them safe.

Evidence that these drugs serve as an effective prophylactic is widespread. For 65 years, chloroquine has been used in Africa and various countries to fight malaria. Where the drug is used regularly, there are no cases of covid-19.

Additionally on a recent talk show two doctors discussed

Hydroxychloroquine, Azithromycin and zinc, in a dose they said costs about $20.00 can be used as a therapeutic cure for those moderately and even severely infected. The sooner one takes the medicine however, the better. Additionally, these doctors treat Lupus patients and Rheumatoid Arthritis Patients with the hydroxychloroquine and have been doing so for years without any patient going to the hospital because of the medicine.

The drug is safe. Additionally, the one doctor treats 2000 patients for Lupus and none have contracted COVID-19. He cited another study of 14,500 Lupus patients and none have COVID. This attests to its prophylaxis capabilities.

Locally on the Frank Andrews show yesterday, Louis called in to tell his story of contracting covid-19. He said he thought he would have no issue because he was young and strong and in good health but after ten days, he had not improved and began having breathing difficulties. After a few days he called 911 and was admitted to treat the coronavirus covid-19.

He was given breathing assistance with a ventilator and he thought he might not make it. Then, he was given Hydroxychloroquine, zinc, and Azithromycin. After a day or so, he was taken off breathing assist and put on oxygen, then a reduced oxygen flow and after a few days he was discharged free of the virus. On death's door to on the way home. That is not anecdotal if you are Louis, that is very real.

A state Democrat representative from Michigan said she heard Donald Trump talking about the possibilities of the drug on TV in one of the updates. She had the virus and was getting worse. She asked her doctor if she could be put on the drug and he did so. In four hours, she told the audience she had no symptoms. Her Doctor was on the air with her.

I am thinking about when the US goes back to work. All of the serology testing for antibodies to see who is immune we know will take forever. America recently brought in 329,000,000 doses of hydroxychloroquine into its stockpile and we are making more. The threat of death is reduced substantially by this drug. When we go back to work, if doctors and the government advocate a prophylaxis of hydroxychloroquine or a cure in case of infection, all of America can go back to work with minimal risk. Don't you think the people in your circulation area of northeastern PA should know about this. Please.

Hospital workers, EMS/EMT workers, Police, Fire. warehouse workers, cashiers, manufacturing workers, etc. -- everybody can be safe rather than sorry.

-- End of 2nd email --

My two favorite antiviral drugs

1. Hydroxychloroquine
2. Remdesivir

An existing, easy-to-produce medicine that proved effective at treating or preventing SARS-CoV-2 infection would provide the fastest relief for patients and doctors. As noted, the early hope is on hydroxychloroquine and chloroquine, and many hospitals, including the University of California,

San Francisco, and the University of Washington, include them in their treatment guidelines. This anti-viral is approved for uses but not as a general treatment for COVID-19. My opinion is that it should have full FDA approval but I am not a doctor. According to the reports, it has saved lives.

1. Hydroxychloroquine, aka Plaquenil

Some doctors are combining hydroxychloroquine with azithromycin, an antibiotic. Much of the published evidence comes from a very small French study and reports from China. Larger, more rigorous clinical trials are starting, but they will take time. Favipiravir, a flu drug shown in Japan, appeared beneficial in another small study. These medicines, especially the malaria drugs, which are being mass-produced, will be used by doctors on the front lines, but we will have to wait for evidence of whether they are benefitting patients and how much.

2. Remdesivir

Timeline: Approved by the FDA in April 2020. Reduces impact of coronavirus by 32% in studies.

From what I have studied, my opinion is that Hydroxychloroquine is more effective.

Remdesivir, an antiviral medicine that failed as an Ebola treatment, was initially developed to work against a different coronavirus. There's some evidence that it benefits Covid-19 patients. Its maker, Gilead, has been working with researchers and governments around the world to get clinical trials up and running.

The company has said to expect results in April. Six large studies are in progress, with the first, in severely ill patients in China. It was due to finish as early as April 3, according to a government website.

A study in patients with milder disease will also finish in April, with two more due in May. In the meantime, Gilead has made the drug available to hundreds of patients on a compassionate use basis.

However, it recently said that, due to overwhelming demand, it would suspend access to the drug for all but pregnant women and children as it works to create a more systematic way of giving it out without interfering with clinical trials. This new system should be in place soon. Remdesivir must be given intravenously.

University of Minnesota tests all-in for hydroxychloroquine

Each day, other than supply, it looks better for hydroxychloroquine. It is getting lots of attention by lots of epidemiologists and the University of Minnesota.

At least three clinical trials for hydroxychloroquine are trying to establish whether the decades-old malaria medication can prevent COVID-19 infections in frontline health-care workers as hospitals across the country scramble to secure enough gowns and masks for their employees.

This includes two clinical trials at the University of Minnesota testing hydroxychloroquine in health care workers reporting pre- and post-exposure to the novel coronavirus. A third trial, funded by a government agency, wants to know if the drug can prevent infections in 15,000 health care workers. See my letter to the editor earlier in this section.

There is growing concern that the current strain on the health care system and its workers isn't sustainable given the high rates of exposure faced by clinicians working in frontline emergency rooms, intensive care units, and newly established COVID-19 units. At the same time, clinicians are being asked to wear one mask per shift or reuse them at some hospitals.

The COVID-19 pandemic has sickened more than 1 million people worldwide, including over 600,000 in the U.S. Over 32,000 people have died in the US. In the U.S., more and more clinicians are contracting the virus, and some are dying.

"The lack of workplace and patient safety right now is catastrophic," Rebecca Givan, an associate professor of labor studies and employment relations at Rutgers University, said in an email.

"Hospitals need to be honest with their workers, and do everything in their power to keep workers safe so that they can continue to provide desperately needed patient care without jeopardizing their own health or that of their families." Hydroxychloroquine can save their employee's lives.

Chapter 7 Serological Testing for Antibodies

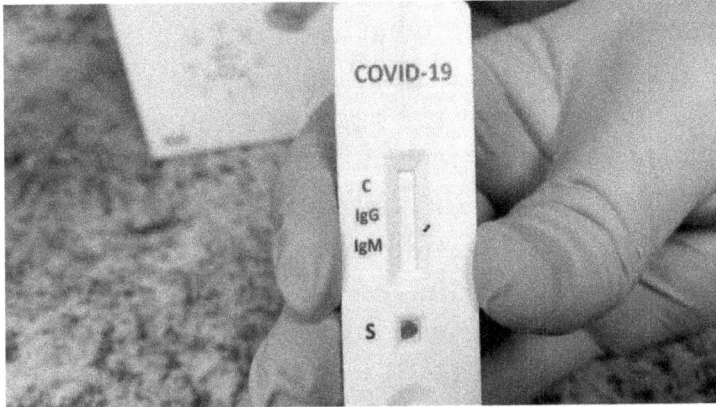

A month ago when President Trump announced that Peter Navarro had procured over 29 million doses of hydroxychloroquine for the storehouse, the drug began to surge out of the storehouses and into pharmacies across the country. Now, just like there was once a shortage of COVID-10 testing and serological testing supplies and the ability to get readouts, there was soon be a shortage of this powerful anti-viral drug and so the stockpile needs to be replaced.

It is my opinion that hydroxychloroquine is vital to the success of an American economic restart. But, the mainstream press who hate anything suggested by Trump have downplayed its use and the demand is not as high. I find it hard to believe that the people believe the press on this one. Doctors are still high on it.

This note is from the Commissioner of Food and Drugs, Food and Drug Administration, Stephen M. Hahn M.D. It explains the tests for antibodies which many beleive will play a role in reopening America. Here is the commissioner's note:

> Serological tests measure the amount of antibodies or proteins present in the blood when the body is responding to a specific infection, like COVID-19. In other words, the test detects the body's immune response to the infection caused by the virus rather than detecting the virus itself. In the early days of an infection when the body's immune response is still building, antibodies may not be detected. This limits the test's effectiveness for diagnosing COVID-19 and why it should not be used as the sole basis to diagnose COVID-19.

> Serological tests can play a critical role in the fight against COVID-19 by helping healthcare professionals to identify individuals who have overcome an infection in the past and have developed an immune response. In the future, this may potentially be used to help determine, together with other clinical data, that such individuals are no longer susceptible to infection and can return to work. In addition, these test results can aid in determining who may donate a part of their blood called convalescent plasma, which may serve as a possible treatment for those who are seriously ill from COVID-19. This is why Vice President Mike Pence called on the laboratory community to develop serological tests for COVID-19.

> In March, the FDA issued a policy to allow developers of certain serological tests to begin to market or use their tests once they have performed the appropriate evaluation to determine that their tests are accurate and reliable. This includes allowing developers to market their tests without prior FDA review if certain conditions

outlined in the guidance document are met. The FDA issued this policy to allow early patient access to certain serological tests with the understanding that the FDA has not reviewed and authorized them.

The FDA can also authorize tests for COVID-19 under an Emergency Use Authorization (EUA). To date, FDA has authorized one EUA for a serological test that is intended for use by clinical laboratories.
Since the FDA issued the policy, over 70 test developers have notified the agency that they have serological tests available for use. However, some firms are falsely claiming that their serological tests are FDA approved or authorized, or falsely claiming that they can diagnose COVID-19. The FDA will take appropriate action against firms making false claims or marketing tests that are not accurate and reliable.

The FDA, an agency within the U.S. Department of Health and Human Services, protects the public health by assuring the safety, effectiveness, and security of human and veterinary drugs, vaccines and other biological products for human use, and medical devices. The agency also is responsible for the safety and security of our nation's food supply, cosmetics, dietary supplements, products that give off electronic radiation, and for regulating tobacco products.

How do we open up America?

One of the approaches to opening up America has to do with seeing who has had the virus in the past so that they can gain a certification to prove that person cannot be infected again. If there were an adequate supply of the antibody tests, this would be difficult to implement on a good day.

The notion of having to prove you're OK to get your freedom to work and walk around certificate may not fly well in a free country. That can be an obstacle as the day gets closer that we open up the country. I think we need a simpler approach. Serology testing may make us feel that we are OK but proving it to an employer or anybody else is going to be problematic. There are after all, 330 million citizens in just America to worry about. There are 7.8 billion worldwide.

There was a headline today that certainly got my attention. It said:

DON'T COUNT ON ANTIBODY TESTS TO REOPEN AMERICA

It offered that blood tests that measure a person's antibodies to the coronavirus could be a powerful tool to determine when it's safe to reopen the country. That is correct.

But after all the good news about the creation and development of such tests, concerns now exist about the accuracy and availability of the tests. Here is how the tests work:

Like the FDA Commissioner said: They detect whether a person has ever been exposed to the virus. But, there are many different tests than the single FDA approved test. These tests are different from those used to diagnose the disease. There are those who believe the existence of all these tests could hamper plans to allow Americans back to work and school.

Entrepreneurial America has created more than 90 different antibody tests. They are all now on the market, but only one has been authorized by the Food and Drug Administration. Why is this? The others "may not be as accurate as we'd like," agency FDA chief Stephen Hahn said recently as talk is ramping up about lifting the shutdown. Hahn's FDA has not verified the other 90 tests as being effective. Surely John Q. Public is not qualified to make this determination.

Public health experts are now warning that just because a person has antibodies to the coronavirus does not necessarily mean that they are immune to the virus, according to David Lim ...... But the antibody testing push comes as President Donald Trump is laser-focused on reopening the economy and governors on both coasts work on plans for a regional restart.

Rhode Island Gov. Gina Raimondo said her administration is already conducting a "deep dive, industry by industry" for guidelines to a "new normal,"

My personal concern is that government can easily guess wrong on who can do what and when in any piecemeal approach to relieving the shutdown. Unlike Dr. Fauci, I advocate turning the switch so we do not have to designate a *grand determinator* at the federal or state level to determine what are the gauntlet points that must be accomplished for a person to be declared free of disease, and then what? ?

So, what do we do about new screening and training for businesses that reopen. What must employees do to qualify? Where do they go? Pennsylvania for example has no testing facilities as of today—no drive throughs. Governor Raimondo is one of six northeast governors working together in a new working group announced Monday. There is a lot of hope for this group but there are a lot of pitfalls. Who makes the decisions for the group if they are independent of the president.

"Everyone is very anxious to get out of the house, get back to work, get the economy moving. Everyone agrees with that," said New York Gov. Andrew Cuomo. "What the art form is going to be here is doing that smartly, and doing that productively, and doing that in a coordinated way."

Chapter 8 The Simplest Formula to Open the Country

Coronavirus' generally held views that happen to be wrong.

The shutdown, lock-down, social distancing, washing hands, masks, gloves, etc. only slows down the virus infection rate. The curve gets flattened but the total area under the curve remains the same over an extended period of time.

Until we reach herd immunity levels of around 65% of the population with antibodies, we don't prevent infections or save more lives. We are only delaying the spread. Total isolation would work.

We could slow the spread rate down if we want until there is a vaccine. That could be next year but that is no silver bullet or guarantee. Less than 50% gets a flu shot every year.

People still get the flu even with the flu shot.

There is no evidence that these measures mandated by the state would be more effective than individual voluntary measures taken by citizens.

Don't you need two populations to compare? One with state mandated measures and one with individual voluntary measures. We do have examples of these two cases and I submit the state imposed are not more effective.

Sweden was voluntary and kept the schools open. Denmark and Norway had state controlled shutdowns with similar results of Sweden. We have eight states with no state shutdown.

'Life Has to Go On': This is why Sweden has faced the virus without a lockdown. The country was an outlier in Europe, trusting its people to voluntarily follow the protocols. Many haven't, but it does not seem to have hurt them. Are the people in Sweden smarter or braver than those in the US? Maybe so! Maybe not! Maybe it is common sense. Sweden has not restricted park use, and bars and restaurants have remained open.

We are not saving any more lives with lockdowns or will have fewer cases until we reach herd immunity.

The idea of flattening the curve was a good one. We didn't run out of hospital rooms or ventilators. The Javits center in NYC only had 50 patients the day after a news reports said they had none. Our citizens flattened the curve not the mandate. In Pennsylvania, Common sense would have worked as well as Governor Wolf and Health Secretary Levine.

If you think the shutdown flattened the curve, where is your proof?

Protect the immune compromised, wear masks, wear gloves, wash your hands and make your own decisions. Allow businesses the same freedom and let individuals make their own decisions regarding the risks.

End of essay

Thank you, Dennis

Comments on Dennis' essay by AL

Dennis has it right. Great, logical, practical. The best writing on this nonsense that I have seen. Nice job Dennis !. Too bad the jerks in Harrisburg (PA) are more interested in destroying Trump and don't care if they also destroy most of America. Why does anyone vote for these phonies ????

Where is the legal grounds for these outrageous decisions ??? I don't think they are legal !

The liberals always think that they know better how your money should be spent, what you should eat and wear, what you should think etc,etc, and they are almost always wrong !

We are not children. We are adults and most adults will make the right decisions. Let the few who refuse to use their heads deal with their consequences. Sure it's a terrible virus and we all need to take precautions. that still won't guarantee that there won't be some painful results. That will happen regardless of any quarantine. But we also need to put 40 plus million people back to work and stop destroying thousands of small business across the country.

No more bailout money and NO money for red states they are broke because of bad management, not the virus. This should not be a time for all the selfish losers in our country to get more money to waste on more stupid ideas. Don't use any of my tax dollars on these jerks !

I think this Governor should be recalled because of his partisan decisions and all the harm he is causing to so many good people in Pennsylvania. I knew when he joined forces with the people in New York and New Jersey, that we were in for a lot of bad decisions.

God help us if the Socialist liberals in Washington ever get back in power - this is only a preview of how they would want to run the country and ruin our lives. Can you say - Venezuela ?

Stay well

Al

Keep It Simple Stupid!

My perspective is to not put a whole load of *gotchas* and *have-tos* , on the public or businesses in order to open after the shutdown. I say" "Let it happen naturally. "The people such as myself and my wife are going to be cautious entering this new open world. Let it up to us make those decisions as to what, and how. The government should just say when! Turn on the light switch now!

We got into this mess because it was unexpected. Nobody knew the risks of droplets or dirty hands or close contact. We have seen the case counts, and the deaths. Only a fool would act haphazardly if the switch were turned back on for the economy to start as of a certain date. We do not need lockdowns or shutdowns or government dictatorial authoritarian rule.

The governors' announcement came several weeks ago as the President asserted that he, not they, would decide when stay-at-home orders could be lifted. It also coincided with news from California Gov. Gavin Newsom, Oregon Gov. Kate Brown and Washington Gov. Jay Inslee that they are working on their own "shared approach" to restarting the West Coast economy and it does not depend on what the East Coast does.

I say let them continue to conspire but all the governors need to immediately set the people free.

Trump, as expected was asked about the governors' efforts during the Monday April 13th Task Force press briefing. Trump was emphatic: "a president's authority is *total*." He added, "And that's the way it's got to be... And the governors know that." Legal scholars say the federal government lacks the power to directly order states to reopen their economies but the Feds have a lot of discretion regarding interstate commerce, which quite frankly, can be anything—even inaction. The last thing America needs is a Constitutional fight before we can open America.

Soon after the president said he was the boss, he decided that the governors should run their own states one by one, one governor at a time. The President in essence backtracked and made the governors of the states the principle decision makers on covid-19 issues including shutdowns, lockdowns, and reopening methodologies.

As noted throughout this book, governors, especially in blue states have often overreached their Consitutional authority and as you can see by the NewsMax survey, 85% of the people are against the governors' persistence in main-taining lockdowns in their states.

Just today, May 14, 2020, Wisconsin's state supreme court ruled that the governor's lockdown was illegal and he nullified the lockdown orders for the state.

Justices on the Wisconsin Supreme Court struck down Democratic Gov. Tony Evers' months long stay-at-home order on Wednesday,. The 4-3 decision marked the first time a state's high court has overturned a governor's stay-at-home order.

Legislative leaders had argued the governor's administration had overstepped its legal authority.

The court rejected the lawmakers' request for a six-day stay to allow the governor to work out new rules, saying the two parties had two weeks since it took up the case to work "in good faith to establish a lawful rule that addresses COVID-19 and its devastating effects on Wisconsin."

"This ruling allows people to once again gather with their loved ones or visit their places of worship without the fear of violating a state order."

In the lawsuit, Republicans contended that Evers and Department of Health Services Secretary Andrea Palm could not continue to extend stay-at-home orders indefinitely without seeking approval from the state legislature.

In writing the majority opinion, the court narrowly that Palm's order "confining all people to their homes, forbidding travel and closing businesses exceeded the statutory authority granted by law to the state's health director during an emergency. This reversed the order giving an unelected Cabinet secretary the power to compel almost 6 million people to stay at home and close their businesses and face imprisonment if they don't comply, with no input from the legislature, without the consent of the people?

I have an answer for Wisconsin and all of the other 49 states in the union. It is simple but logical and it will work.

The simplest formula to open the country

Today is May 15, 2020. If I were in charge of the reopening of America, this would be the recommended approach:

It is based on the supposition that every living person has a desire to survive. These are the steps after the governor decides to turn the GO SWITCH to ON. The state is not involved in the solution. In other words, the formula is a guideline for the people to follow. There would be no penalties for non-compliance other than the normal laws of the states. Here goes:

1. Businesses should make the changes necessary to promote

a safe workplace so that employees feel safe and customers will frequent the establishment.

2. All employees preparing to go back to work or already working or those people planning to not stay in 100% lockdown should first see their doctor or clinician first; discuss their plans; schedule a test, and if you do not have antibodies, ask your provider for a prescription for the hydroxychloroquine prophylaxis. If your physician has a better recommendation than Hydrochloroquine, Azithromycin, & Zinc, ask the provider for a prophylaxis dosage.

3. States need to designate areas for serology and disease testing and medicine dispensing. Tests are much more available in all states and so this should not be a challenge. Call your local radio station or a help line to find out where to get your testing. Hydroxychloroquine prophylaxis needs to be made available for those who ask for it to be their prime prophylaxis and curative solution. Patients should be able to get their dosages at:

A. Doctors Offices
B. Clinics
C. Private Urgent Care facilities
D. Additional Facilities such as pharmacies and private areas staffed by PAs and / or nurses.
E. Doctor / Med professional recommended prophylaxis should be taken by all workers who feel the need to wear masks.

4. Shutdown is lifted across the country immediately. Today is May 14, 2020.

5. Behavioral recommendations (not mandatory) are

continued

Social distancing , hand washing etc. Avoid contact if not necessary. A new rule book of how to stay safe should be put together and made available free to all citizens online or in paper form.

6. All businesses, entertainment, including restaurants, plays, movies, gymnasiums, swimming pools, parks, etc. may open. People need to voluntarily exercise caution like during the shutdown to avoid crowds if possible. If a place is crowded, go someplace else. If you are sick, stay home

7. Mass transportation reopens. Transit workers take prophylaxis. Riders use masks and recommended precautions

8. Face masks recommended in public until further notice but not mandatory

9. People should stay at home except when they decide to go out to parks, for walks, movies or dinner, etc. There are no restrictions on visiting neighbors or family other than in hospitals and nursing homes.

10. Employees will be called back to work by employers. They would have five to ten days to report to work. Those fearful to return to work may request up to 30 days additional leave. Unemployment compensation for those choosing the thirty day call-back to work should continue perhaps at a reduced rate.

Summary

Instead of the government determining what is best for the

people, the people have already suffered, some for almost ten weeks with the country in lockdown. The people are not stupid. We understand the risks of the virus by now. The people are naturally cautious and authoritative restrictions will not make us more cautious.

Over time, we may choose to brave the outside world when we feel the time is right. Plus, we may opt to dine inside a restaurant with or without a prophylaxis such as hydroxychloroquine. The medicine would serve as a crutch so that we would not be infected. Use similar prophylaxis cautions to protect yourself from infection.

I would recommend taking the proper amount of a prophylaxis such as hydroxychloroquine to ward off the virus. This dosage medicine may last about three weeks or perhaps longer. Renew the prophylaxis regimen as required. Ask your provider. This would be more effective than the antibodies testing and the drug can be made more available than the test. The idea is that eventually the coronavirus will be gone.

If you think you have contracted the virus or are concerned about it, you should get tested wherever you can. If positive, ask the physician or attendant for a prescription for hydroxychloroquine with a packet of Zinc and another prescription for Azythromycin. This three pack has been effective in curing the virus in some people. It can cure the virus but it is not 100% guaranteed.

Go home and quarantine for 14 days while taking the medicine at the recommended dosage(often 5 days) until the doctor says you no longer have the virus. If you do not improve, call your doctor. Like all medicine, nothing is 100% but hydroxychloroquine is one that I will be looking for if I get sick.

It should be part of the nations recommended solution for reopening. Again, other solutions such as Remdesivir can also be effective. Consult your physician.

By all means reopen the country so we have an economy ready to go when we as a country are finally ready to stop hibernating. This is America and we have a Constitution. No state or federal official can superimpose their will on the people.

Other Books by Brian W. Kelly: (amazon.com, and Kindle)

CORONAVIRUS The Cause & the Cure. Many solutions—but which ones will work?
Great Moments in Kansas City Chiefs Football. From the beginning to the Andy Reid Era
How the Philadelphia Eagles Lost Its Karma. This is the one place that tells the story
Cancel All Student Debt Now! Good for America, Good for the Economy.
Social Security Screw Job!!! Scandal: Seniors Intentionally Screwed by US Government
Trump Hate They hate Trump Supporters; Trump; & God—in that order
Christmas Wings for Brian A heartwarming story of a boy whose shoulders kept growing
Merry Christmas to Wilkes-Barre 50 Ways" for Mayor George Brown to Create a Better City.
Air Force Football Championship Seasons From AF Championship to Coach Calhoun's latest team
Syracuse Football Championship Seasons beginning of SU championships; goes to Dino Babers Era
Navy Football Championship Seasons 1ˢᵗ Navy Championships to the Ken Niumatalolo Era
Army Football Championship Seasons Beginning of Football championships to Jeff Monken Era
Florida Gators Championship Seasons Beginning of Football through championships to Dan Mullen era
Alabama's Championship Seasons Beginning of Football past the 2017/2018 National Championship
Clemson Tigers Championship Seasons Beginning of Football to the Clemson National Championships
Penn State's Championship Seasons PSU's first championship to the James Franklin era
Notre Dame's Championship Seasons Before Knute Rockne and past Lou Holtz's 1988 undisputed title
Super Bowls & Championship Seasons: The New York Giants Many championships of the Giants.
Super Bowls & Championship Seasons: New England Patriots Many championships of the Patriots.
Super Bowls & Championship Seasons: The Pittsburgh Steelers Many championship of the Steelers.
Super Bowls & Championship Seasons: The Philadelphia Eagles Many championships of the Eagles.
The Big Toxic School Wilkes-Barre Area's Tale of Corruption, Deception, Taxation & Tyranny
Great Players in New York Giants Football Begins with great players of 1925 to the Saquon Barqley era.
Great Coaches in New York Giants Football Begins with Bob Folwell 1925 and to Pat Shurmur in 2019.
Great Moments in New York Giants Football Beginning of Football to the Pat Shurmur era.
Hasta La Vista California Give California its independence.
IT's ALL OVER! Mueller: "NO COLLUSION!"—Top Dems going to jail for the hoax!
Democrat Secret for Power & Winning Elections Open borders adds millions of new Democrat Voters
Hope for Wilkes-Barre—John Q. Doe—Next Mayor of Wilkes-Barre
The John Doe Plan & WB Plan will help create a better city!
Great Moments in New England Patriots Football Second Edition
This book begins at the beginning of Football and goes to the Bill Belichick era.
The Cowardly Congress Corrupt US Congress is against America and Americans.
Great Players in Air Force Football From the beginning to the current season
Great Coaches in Air Force Football Grom the beginning to Coach Troy Calhoun
Help for Mayor George and Next Mayor of Wilkes-Barre How to vote for the next Mayor Council
Ghost of Wilkes-Barre Future: Spirit's advice for residents how to pick the next Mayor and Council
Great Players in Air Force Football: Air Force's best players of all time
Great Coaches in Air Force Football: From Coach 1 to Coach Troy Calhoun
Great Moments in Air Force Football: From day 1 to today
Great Players in Navy Football: Navy's best including Bellino & Staubach
Great Coaches in Navy Football: From Coach 1 to Coach #39 Ken Niumatalolo
Great Moments in Navy Football: From day 1 to coach Ken Niumatalolo l
No Tree! No Toys! No Toot! Heartwarming story. Christmas gone while 19 month old napped
How to End DACA, Sanctuary Cities, & Resident Illegal Aliens . best solution remove shadowsAmerica.
Government Must Stop Ripping Off Seniors' Social Security!: Hey buddy, seniors can't spare a dime?
Special Report: Solving America's Student Debt Crisis!: The only real solution to the $1.52 Trillion debt
The Winning Political Platform for America Unique winning approach to solve big problems in America.
Lou Barletta v Bob Casey for US Senate Barletta's unique approach to solve big problems in America.
John Chrin v Matt Cartwright for Congress Chrin has a unique approach to solve big problems in America.
The Cure for Hate !!! Can the cure be any worse than this disease that is crippling America?
Andrew Cuomo's Time to Go? "He Was Never that Great!"**:** Cuomo says America never that great
White People Are Bad! Bad! Bad! Whoever thought a popular slogan in 2018 *It's OK to be White!*
The Fake News Media Is Also Corrupt !!! Fake press / media today is not worthy to be 4ᵗʰ Estate.
God Gave US Donald Trump? Trump was sent from God as the people's answer
Millennials Say America Was "Never That Great": Too many pleased days of political chumps not over!
It's Time for The John Q. Doe Party… Don't you think? By Elephants.
<u>**Great Players in Florida Gators Football**… Tim Tebow and a ton of other great players</u>
Great Coaches in Florida Gators Football… The best coaches in Gator history.
The Constitution by Hamilton, Jefferson, Madison, et al. The Real Constitution
The Constitution Companion. Will help you learn and understand the Constitution
Great Coaches in Clemson Football The best Clemson Coaches right to Dabo Swinney
Great Players in Clemson Football The best Clemson players in history
Winning Back America. America's been stolen and can be won back completely
The Founding of America… Great book to pick up a lot of great facts
Defeating America's Career Politicians. The scoundrels need to go.
Midnight Mass by Jack Lammers… You remember what it was like Great story
The Bike by Jack Lammers… Great heartwarming Story by Jack
Wipe Out All Student Loan Debt--Now! Watch the economy go boom!
No Free Lunch Pay Back Welfare! Why not pay it back?
Deport All Millennials Now!!! Why they deserve to be deported and/or saved
DELETE the EPA, Please! The worst decisions to hurt America
Taxation Without Representation 4ᵗʰ Edition Should we throw the TEA overboard again?
Four Great Political Essays by Thomas Dawson
Top Ten Political Books for 2018… Cliffnotes Version of 10 Political Books

Top Six Patriotic Books for 2018... Cliffnotes version of 6 Patriotic Boosk
Why Trump Got Elected!.. It's great to hear about a great milestone in America!
The Day the Free Press Died. Corrupt Press Lives on!
Solved (Immigration) The best solutions for 2018
Solved II (Obamacare, Social Security, Student Debt) Check it out; They're solved.
Great Moments in Pittsburgh Steelers Football... Six Super Bowls and more.
Great Players in Pittsburgh Steelers Football ,,,Chuck Noll, Bill Cowher, Mike Tomin, etc.
Great Coaches in New England Patriots Football,,, Bill Belichick the one and only plus others
Great Players in New England Patriots Football... Tom Brady, Drew Bledsoe et al.
Great Coaches in Philadelphia Eagles Football..Andy Reid, Doug Pederson & Lots more
Great Players in Philadelphia Eagles Football Great players such as Sonny Jurgenson
Great Coaches in Syracuse Football All the greats including Ben Schwartzwalder
Great Players in Syracuse Football. Highlights best players such as Jim Brown & Donovan McNabb
Millennials are People Too !!! Give US millennials help to live American Dream
Brian Kelly for the United States Senate from PA: Fresh Face for US Senate
The Candidate's Bible. Don't pray for your campaign without this bible
Rush Limbaugh's Platform for Americans... Rush will love it
Sean Hannity's Platform for Americans... Sean will love it
Donald Trump's New Platform for Americans. Make Trump unbeatable in 2020
Tariffs Are Good for America! One of the best tools a president can have
Great Coaches in Pittsburgh Steelers Football Sixteen of the best coaches ever to coach in pro football.
Great Moments in New England Patriots Football Great football moments from Boston to New England
Great Moments in Philadelphia Eagles Football. The best from the Eagles from the beginning of football.
Great Moments in Syracuse Football The great moments, coaches & players in Syracuse Football
Boost Social Security Now! Hey Buddy Can You Spare a Dime?
The Birth of American Football. From the first college game in 1869 to the last Super Bowl
Obamacare: A One-Line Repeal Congress must get this done.
A Wilkes-Barre Christmas Story A wonderful town makes Christmas all the better
A Boy, A Bike, A Train, and a Christmas Miracle A Christmas story that will melt your heart
Pay-to-Go   America-First Immigration Fix
Legalizing Illegal Aliens Via Resident Visas Americans-first plan saves $Trillions. Learn how!
60 Million Illegal Aliens in America!!! A simple, America-first solution.
The Bill of Rights By Founder James Madison Refresh *your knowledge of the specific rights for all*
Great Players in Army Football Great Army Football played by great players..
Great Coaches in Army Football Army's coaches are all great.
Great Moments in Army Football Army Football at its best.
Great Moments in Florida Gators Football Gators Football from the start. This is the book.
Great Moments in Clemson Football CU Football at its best. This is the book.
Great Moments in Florida Gators Football Gators Football from the start. This is the book.
The Constitution Companion. A Guide to Reading and Comprehending the Constitution
The Constitution by Hamilton, Jefferson, & Madison – Big type and in English
PATERNO: The Dark Days After Win # 409. Sky began to fall within days of win # 409.
JoePa 409 Victories: Say No More! Winningest Division I-A football coach ever
American College Football: The Beginning From before day one football was played.
Great Coaches in Alabama Football Challenging the coaches of every other program!
Great Coaches in Penn State Football the Best Coaches in PSU's football program
Great Players in Penn State Football The best players in PSU's football program
Great Players in Notre Dame Football The best players in ND's football program
Great Coaches in Notre Dame Football The best coaches in any football program
Great Players in Alabama Football from Quarterbacks to offensive Linemen Greats!
Great Moments in Alabama Football AU Football from the start. This is the book.
Great Moments in Penn State Football PSU Football, start--games, coaches, players,
Great Moments in Notre Dame Football ND Football, start, games, coaches, players
Cross Country with the Parents A great trip from East Coast to West with the kids
Seniors, Social Security & the Minimum Wage. Things seniors need to know.
How to Write Your First Book and Publish It with CreateSpace. You too can be an author.
The US Immigration Fix--It's all in here. Finally, an answer!
I had a Dream IBM Could be #1 Again The title is self-explanatory
WineDiets.Com Presents The Wine Diet Learn how to lose weight while having fun.
Wilkes-Barre, PA; Return to Glory Wilkes-Barre City's return to glory
Geoffrey Parsons' Epoch... The Land of Fair Play Better than the original.
The Bill of Rights 4 Dummmies! This is the best book to learn about your rights.
Sol Bloom's Epoch ...Story of the Constitution The best book to learn the Constitution
America 4 Dummmies! All Americans should read to learn about this great country.
The Electoral College 4 Dummmies! How does it really work?
The All-Everything Machine Story about IBM's finest computer server.
ThankYou IBM! This book explains how IBM was beaten in the computer marketplace by neophytes

Amazon.com/author/brianwkelly

Brian W. Kelly has written 225 books including this one.

Thank you for buying this one.

Others can be found at amazon.com/author/brianwkelly

www.ingramcontent.com/pod-product-compliance
Lightning Source LLC
Chambersburg PA
CBHW070928280326
41934CB00009B/1786